Written by Kirsten

SEM photos by Dennis Kunkel Microscopy, Inc.

Illustrated and designed by Dan Jankowski

Initial design and idea presented by
University of Central Florida Graphic Design Students:
Crystal Bell, Sarah Eshleman, Benjamin Miles

an imprint of
📚 SCHOLASTIC
www.scholastic.com

Scholastic and Tangerine Press and associated logos
are trademarks of Scholastic Inc.

Published by Tangerine Press, an imprint of Scholastic Inc.,
557 Broadway; New York, NY 10012

Scholastic Australia Pty. Ltd   Scholastic New Zealand Ltd.   Scholastic Canada Ltd.
Gosford, NSW   Greenmount, Auckland   Markham, Ontario
                                     10 9 8 7 6 5 4 3 2 1

ISBN-10: 0-545-13583-4

ISBN-13: 978-0-545-13583-2

Made in China

"Beware of these guys and gals!"

"The grossest of all!"

"Stingers and biters"

"The ultimate pests"

"Collect your own critters!"

The word microscope comes from the Greek words "micron," which means "small," and "scopein," which means "to look at."

Up Close...
Now Eye See!

Everything in this world is made up of smaller parts that you can't see. That's where a microscope comes in handy! This little marvel was invented more than 400 years ago. With a microscope, even the cells of your body become visible!

There are three different kinds of microscopes:

Optical Theory Microscopes

Electron Microscopes

Scanning Probe Microscopes

The type of microscope you've seen on your science teacher's desk is the *optical theory microscope*. (It's also the kind that came packaged with this book—which happens to be a handheld model, making it extra portable for on-the-go-examinations!)

Optical microscopes focus light with the help of two curved, refractive lenses made of glass or plastic. A *refractive lens* bends the light that passes through it. Most optical microscopes used today can make an image look up to 1,000 times its actual size!

Have you ever noticed that your legs appear much smaller or bigger than they really are when you look down at them in a swimming pool? If so, you have seen refraction in action. As the light passes through the water, it's bent. Suddenly, what you're looking at appears differently.

4

The incredible close-up insect images you see in this book were taken with *scanning electron microscopes* (also called SEMs). Unlike regular microscopes, which use glass lenses to bend light waves, SEMs use *electrons* (negatively charged particles). With an SEM, you'll get a much more detailed image than you would with an optical microscope. Even better, SEM images are three-dimensional!

Before an insect can be viewed with an SEM, it must be dried out (so it doesn't shrink and shrivel) and dusted in a coating of gold (which conducts electricity).

Antony van Leeuwenhoek (lay-ven-hook) of Holland is referred to as "the father of microscopy." He invented the world's first simple microscope by grinding and polishing tiny curved lenses. He was able to make things he looked at hundreds of times larger than they actually were.

My Name Is...
Since 1735, animals and plants have been organized in a system called *Linnaean taxonomy*. Each belongs to a group based on what it look likes and/or how it behaves. You'll see the family name or the genus and species names for each critter in this book.

...And Gross!

Entomology 101

An *entomologist* studies insects. To an entomologist, an insect isn't gross—it's fascinating!

Do you think you have what it takes to be an entomologist? Test yourself to find out!

Which of the following statements about insects are true?

A) They are members of the animal kingdom.

B) They are invertebrates (they lack backbones).

C) They have exoskeletons (these are hard skeletons on their outsides).

D) They are important to animals that eat them.

E) All of the above!

If you guessed E, you already know quite a bit about insects!

But did you also know that ...

There are so many kinds of insects out there that we don't even have names for at least 4 million of them?

More than 70 percent of all Earth's animals are insects?

Without insects, much of our plant life on this planet would die?

An insect's blood is clear, pale yellow, or green?

Insects don't have lungs or breathe through their mouths?

BODY BASICS

When you look at an insect through a microscope, expect to see features that will surprise you. You may be shocked to discover that some bugs have hair. Others have multiple eyes. And some have really freaky fangs!

An insect's body is made up of three separate parts:

Thorax: An insect's wings and legs are attached to its thorax.

Abdomen: Some insect abdomens contain tails, stingers, or *cerci* (sensors). Insects' digestive systems, hearts, and reproductive organs are housed here.

Head: This is where you will see an insect's eyes, mouthparts, and antennae.

Insects are arthropods. Arthropods have hard coverings (called *exoskeletons*) on the outside of their segmented bodies. Like insects, arachnids (such as spiders and scorpions) are also arthropods. But arachnids are not insects, even though they're often mistaken for them.

Bug blood is also called *hemolymph* (hee-muh-limf).

7

Praying mantis kung fu is based on the way a mantis defends itself aggressively from other insects, even much larger ones.

Danger!

In the insect world, danger is everywhere. When insects are not protecting themselves from bigger animals (which includes just about every other animal!), they're battling other insects.

Insects have developed different methods of protecting themselves. Some blend in with their surroundings. Others are escape artists. Still others prefer to fight back.

SAFE AND SOUND

How do insects stay safe in the presence of danger?

- **THEY RUN!** Cockroaches run in fast, short spurts. Try to catch one and see for yourself!

- **THEY JUMP!** A grasshopper's hind legs are long and strong, which helps it make large leaps.

- **THEY FLY!** A great fly-catching tip: Houseflies always take off in the air backward.

- **THEY ROLL!** The golden wheel spider "cartwheels" its way across a dune to shake its enemies.

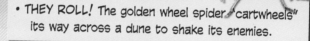

- **THEY TASTE GROSS!** Birds or other creatures that eat Monarch butterflies usually spit them right back out or throw them up later.

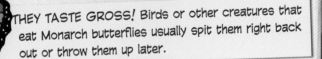

- **THEY STAB!** New Guinea walking sticks stab predators with super-sharp spines.

- **THEY STINK!** A shield bug's scent can stick around for days.

- **THEY CAMOUFLAGE!** Leaf-bugs blend in with the leaves, whether standing still or swaying in the breeze.

- **THEY MIMIC!** Some moth species have spots on their wings that look like large eyes.

Butterflies

Genus: *Asterocampa*

Species: More than 20,000 kinds throughout the world

The painted lady butterfly flies between Africa and Iceland, a distance of nearly 4,000 mi. (6,437 km)!

The butterfly is a particularly slow flier—one of the slowest flying insects, in fact. Its four large, scaled wings beat about 10 times a second. Compare that to the housefly, whose wings beat 190 times per second, and the honeybee, who has a wing beat rate of 250 per second!

Predators sometimes leave butterflies alone because of their brightly colored wings. A general rule in the insect world: A critter's bright colors mean it tastes foul or is toxic.

Some butterflies use camouflage to protect themselves. They sit atop other brightly colored objects, including flowers. Others *mimic* (imitate) dangerous animals in order to stay safe. The spots on a butterfly's wings may be confused with the wide eyes of bigger animals.

PRESTO, CHANGE-O!

Butterflies go through what is called *metamorphosis* (met-uh-mawr-fuh-sis) when they change from babies to adults. Here's how it happens:

1. A butterfly begins its life as an egg.

2. It hatches into a caterpillar larva.

3. The larva eats and eats to get big and strong.

4. The larva burrows underground or attaches itself to a food source.

5. It lives for a while (and changes) inside of a cocoon.

6. It comes out of its cocoon as a full-grown adult.

7. Its wings open, expand, and dry.

8. Off it flies!

A butterfly uses its *proboscis* to suck up nectar and other liquids (including sweat and urine!). Its proboscis is coiled up when the butterfly isn't eating.

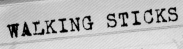

WALKING STICKS

Family: Heteronemiidae

The small hairs on the walking stick's antennae are used to sense changes in the air.

A walking stick egg is the largest egg of any insect at ½ in. (1.27 cm) in length. That's about the size of your pinky fingernail.

The stick insect protects itself by mimicking sticks. The scientific name for this insect group is *phasmid*. In Latin, phasmid means "phantom." Phantom is another word for ghost. The walking stick doesn't have any sort of obvious body, so it's easy to see why it was given this name.

Some walking sticks escape their predators by camouflaging with nearby sticks and twigs. Others spray the eyes and mouths of predators with a substance that causes a burning sensation.

PET PESTS

Some people keep stick insects as pets. Stick insects are easy to care for. All a walking stick pet owner needs is:

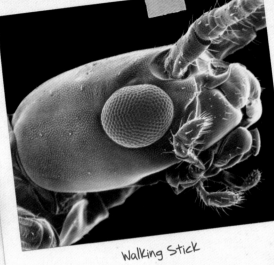

Walking Stick

- A tall jar and lid (with air holes)

- A room set at a comfortable temperature

- Plants for feeding (such as ivy and lettuce)

When stick insects molt (shed their old skin), they sometimes eat the dead skin!

The giant walking stick is more than 1 ft. (3 m) long, making it the longest insect in the world. It lives in the rain forests of Indonesia.

AND GROSS

WALKING STICKS

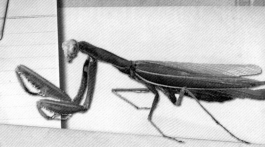

MANTIDS

Genus: *Stagomantis*

Species: *carolina*

There are more than 2,300 mantid species worldwide. Mantids get their name from the Greek word *mantis*, which means "prophet" or "fortune teller." Mantids earned the name because of the way they stand. A standing mantid looks like a person in prayer.

Praying mantises use camouflage to blend in with its surroundings. Sometimes they match the colors of nearby plants. They mimic other objects, such as a leaf or mushroom. A mantid may even disguise itself as bird droppings!

Mantids are excellent hunters. They hold their prey tightly with their *pincers* (claws). Sometimes they even eat their victims while they are still alive.

ON THE MENU

Favorite mantid snacks include:

- Insects
- Frogs
- Birds
- Lizards
- Rodents
- Snakes

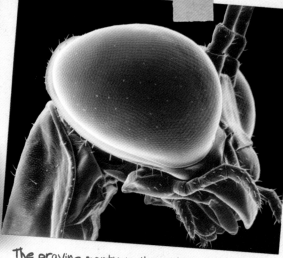

The praying mantis is the only insect that can turn its head from side to side.

A flower mantis may look so much like a flower that another insect will land atop it while searching for nectar.

A praying mantis uses these spikes on its forelegs to seize its prey.

MANTIDS

15

GIANT WATER BUGS

Genus: *Lethocerus*

A giant water bug's beak is strong—and its bite is painful!

Most giant water bugs live in streams and ponds in North America, South America, and Asia. When it's time to hunt for food, they dive deep toward the water's floor. Because they need oxygen to breathe, they carry bubbles of air from the water's surface down with them. Then, they wait motionless for prey to come near.

When a giant water bug strikes, it injects its victim with a special kind of saliva. The saliva turns the victim's insides into liquid. Then, the giant water bug drinks its meal.

Giant water bugs are sometimes called "toe biters." Have you ever felt one nibble on your feet while they dangled in water? Lucky for us, giant water bugs prefer the taste of other animals.

MR. MOM

And the Father of the Year award goes to...the giant water bug! A giant water bug mom will glue up to 100 fertilized eggs to the father's back. Then, she'll take off. It's Dad's job to care for the eggs until they hatch. He carries them around with him everywhere. He makes sure that they get enough sunlight and water. Sometimes, he even rocks the eggs!

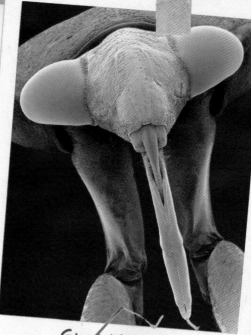

Giant Water Bug

Don't be surprised if you're offered a giant water bug as a snack in Thailand—it's a popular Thai Treat!

GIANT WATER BUGS

MILLIPEDES

Family: Parajulidae

Species: About 10,000 different kinds

Millipedes are arthropods, but they're not insects.

The millipede gets its name from the Latin roots *milli* (which means "thousand") and *ped* (which means "foot"). Even though a millipede doesn't actually have a thousand legs, some species do have up to 750 of them. Others, however, have as few as 24.

Don't confuse millipedes with centipedes! Millipedes have two pairs of legs per body segment, but centipedes have just one pair of legs per body segment. Another difference is that millipedes move slowly, while centipedes are much faster.

When a millipede needs to escape from someone or something, this slow runner knows better than to try to run away. Instead, it forces its way into the ground, moving its body like a wave.

DID YOU KNOW?

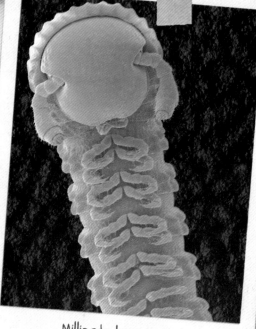

Millipede legs up close!

- Baby millipedes eat their parents' poop to get the nutrition they need.

- One kind of millipede can jump 1 in. (2.5 cm) in the air when startled.

- Some millipedes spray their enemies in the eyes and mouth with a toxic liquid.

- A millipede has short legs. It's a slow walker—but a fast digger!

The largest millipede is the giant African millipede. It can grow up to 1 ft. (3 m) long and be as thick as your thumb!

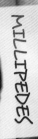

MILLIPEDES

BLOOD BROTHERS

Hostage Takers

Some bugs aren't afraid of people and animals. In fact, they hunt us!

Insects that feed on blood are hematophagous (hee-muh-tof-uh-guhs). Many arthropods and worms are hematophagous. Two of the most common types are bedbugs and leeches.

The Bedbug

The bedbug is a perfect example of a hostage-taker. Bedbugs are small creatures that hunt for blood at nighttime. Bedbugs like warm victims—so it makes sense that they hunt underneath blankets. You might not feel a bedbug bite until hours later!

The Leech

A leech attaches itself to its host and drinks until it's full. Then, it falls off and digests the blood it drank. Leeches have special suckers that release numbing chemicals into their victims, making it impossible to feel a leech at work.

Critters that live on larger animals and depend on them for food are called *parasites*. The larger animal is called the *host*.

The tapeworm is another type of hostage-taker. Unlike some of the "blood brothers" you just met, the tapeworm works inside its host's body—especially in the intestines.

Tapeworms live in animals and are sometimes eaten by accident in undercooked meat. A tapeworm can grow up to 50 ft. (15-0.25 m) long and may live up to 20 years!

21

LICE

Genus: *Pediculus*

Species: *P. humanus*

A head louse measures about 0.8-.12 in. (2-3 mm) in length—about the size of a sesame seed. Head lice live on the heads of people, right where the hair meets the scalp. They can travel from one person to another when heads touch. They are also passed between hosts by pillows, hats, headphones, and hairbrushes.

The life of a louse is a simple one. It's born atop its host. It lives atop its host. And it dies atop its host!

Lice don't have wings, and they can't jump. They can't go far on their own, which is why they cling to their hosts.

Lice live in hair, fur, and feathers. When a louse hatches out of an egg, it pierces its host's skin with its mouth. Then, it begins to suck its victim's blood.

If a louse falls off its host, it will die. It needs its victim's warm body and blood in order to survive.

THERE ARE MANY DIFFERENT KINDS OF LOUSE, INCLUDING:

Body lice: These lice live on clothing, but they move onto a host's skin when it's time to feed.

Chewing lice: Snack-time favorites for these lice include dead skin flakes and feathers.

Sucking lice: Sucking lice are usually found in the fine hair of children.

The claws of this head louse are used to cling to its victim.

LICE

FLEAS

Family: Hystrichopsyllidae

Species: More than 2,000 different
kinds

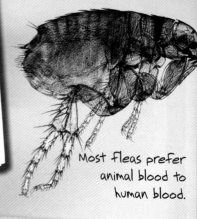

Most fleas prefer
animal blood to
human blood.

Fleas are excellent jumpers. The rubbery pads on their knees help to spring them into the air. Fleas can jump as high as 7 in. (18 cm) and as far as 13 in. (33 cm)!

Fleas use their bristles and spines to attach themselves to their hosts. Once a flea anchors itself onto an animal's fur or feathers, it's very tough to remove.

Most fleas feed on the blood of mammals. Some fleas also pester birds. A victim may try to bite, claw, or peck off these nasty pests. But a flea's body is so sturdy that it can't be easily crushed.

EASY AS 1, 2, 3!

Here's how a flea feeds:

1. It spies skin and lands on it.

2. It tilts its head down and angles its butt up.

3. It stabs its head into the skin and sucks blood.

Fleas can spread diseases between people and animals. In the 14th century, millions of people in Europe and Asia died from an illness called *bubonic plague*, which was spread from rats to humans by—you guessed it—fleas.

A flea's mouthparts are shaped like tubes and are used to suck.

FLEAS

MITES

Family: Demodicidae

Species: About 40,000 different kinds throughout the world (and hundreds of thousands more that are still unidentified!)

A sarcoptic mange mite is a dog's worst enemy. If Rover manages to get a sarcoptic mange mite, he'll itch like crazy and probably lose a lot of his fur!

Mites have been around for about 400 million years. Some live in soil and water. Others live on plants and animals. Mites sometimes even survive by eating mold.

Mites are so small that they're rarely seen, but they're found in many places, especially warm and humid ones—like your bed!

The house dust mite is the most familiar type of mite. The demodex mite is the kind that lives on hair follicles. These critters make hosts out of both animals and people.

Some people are allergic to mites, whose bites can cause hay fever, asthma, and skin conditions such as eczema.

PET PEST

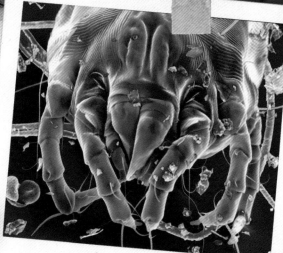

The demodex mite feeds on skin flakes and oil with its pinlike mouthparts.

D GROSS

The Archegozetes longise-tosus is an incredibly strong creature. This tropical mite can lift up to 1,182 times its own weight. That would be like you lifting five adult elephants!

MITES

TICKS

Families: Ixodidae (hard ticks)
and Argasidae (soft ticks)

Ticks are either hard or soft. The hard tick spends quite a bit of time atop its host. Some hard ticks stay with their hosts for their entire lifetime! Soft ticks spend much less time visiting their victims; they prefer to eat and run.

Ticks hunt for their hosts. They climb onto plants and wait for passing victims. These critters are very difficult to remove once they've attached themselves to a victim's skin.

LOOK OUT!

Deer ticks live in forests, hunting for white-tailed deer. A female deer tick will drink its victim's blood for four days. Once she's finally full, she'll drop off and fall onto the ground. Deer ticks can carry diseases, like Lyme disease.

Ticks wave their arms in the air when they're ready to catch a ride on a host.

Grim Reapers

Other insects—such as mosquitoes and flies—spread diseases, too. They cause harm to humans and animals.

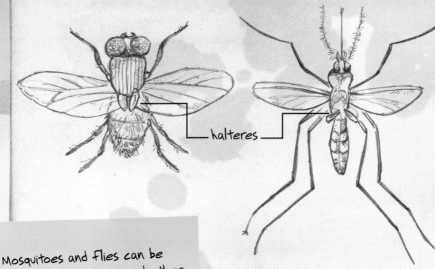

halteres

Mosquitoes and flies can be really annoying to us and other animals, but the little buggers are big helpers when it comes to our planet! They pollinate plants, and they serve as meals for other animals, including some fish.

Mosquitoes and flies are true flies. True flies have two sets of wings, but only one is used for flying. The other two wings are called *halteres*, which help the bugs keep their balance while in the air.

PUBLIC ENEMIES

Mosquitoes and flies are just two of many insects that spread disease. Meet this other grim reaper threesome:

The Sandfly: Sandflies live in sandy places. Their bites can transmit a disease known as *leishmaniasis*. A person with leishmaniasis may suffer skin sores, fever, and even organ damage.

The Black Fly: The black fly is a relative of the mosquito. Female black flies suck animal blood, while males prefer nectar. Black flies live in North and South America and Africa. They spread diseases such as river blindness, which can damage an animal's eye.

The Tsetse Fly: This large African fly measures about $\frac{1}{2}$ in. (1.27 cm) in length. Tsetse flies spread a disease called *sleeping sickness*. People with sleeping sickness suffer fevers and headaches. If it's not treated, sleeping sickness can be deadly. Tsetse fly bites can also cause a person's joints to hurt.

FLIES

Genus: *Musca*

Species: *M. domestica*

A fly's eye is made up of thousands of individual lenses.

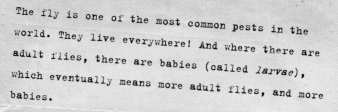

The fly is one of the most common pests in the world. They live everywhere! And where there are adult flies, there are babies (called *larvae*), which eventually means more adult flies, and more babies.

Flies move in all directions. They can fly forward, backward, and from side to side. A fly can turn itself in a complete circle in the air. Sometimes a fly doesn't actually move anywhere—it just beats its wings to hover in one place.

Flies feed on anything they can find—including dead animals and dung! Fly larvae can chew their food. Adults can't, so they suck and lick their meals instead.

TRUE OR FALSE?

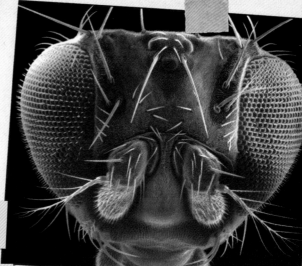

1. Houseflies have tiny hairs on their feet. _____

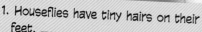

2. They always take off backward. _____

3. They walk on ceilings with the help of their tongues. _____

4. Their buzzing is actually a form of singing. _____

5. They have been around for close to 65 million years. _____

6. They carry diseases that can kill. _____

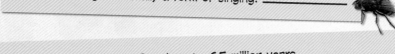

7. They rub their legs together to "clean" them. _____

FLIES

MOSQUITOES

Family: Culicidae

Species: About 3,000 different
kinds throughout the world

A male mosquito's antennae are covered in little featherlike hairs.

Mosquitoes sometimes carry a deadly disease called malaria. They can also carry yellow fever and West Nile Virus.

The mosquito gets its name from the Spanish language. In Spanish, mosquito means "little fly."

Most mosquitoes are nocturnal. This means that they fly around in the evening and at dawn. During the day, they usually rest in cool places.

Mosquitoes rarely travel far from where they were born. When they do, it's usually because they were blown by the wind.

A dragonfly can eat up to 100 mosquitoes in just one day!

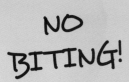

NO BITING!

Wonder why you get an itchy red bump wherever a mosquito bites you? It's because your body is allergic to a mosquito's saliva.

You don't need to worry about male mosquitoes—it's the females who bite! First, she'll pierce a hole in your skin with her mouthparts. Then, she'll suck up your blood through a long needle made of tubes called *stylets*. Her saliva will keep your blood thin while she slurps away.

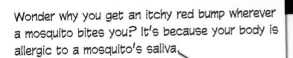

GROSS

MOSQUITOES

Garbage Grazers

Some insects just aren't picky about where they live or what they eat. Garbage grazers live in and eat some really gross stuff—including trash and poop! Check it out:

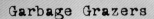

- Blowflies: Adult blowflies feed on flower nectar. But their babies don't have quite the same good taste. Baby blowflies would rather eat garbage and animal remains!

- Lacewing larvae: These critters more than earn their "trash bug" nickname. They are known to cover themselves with garbage when hiding from predators. Sometimes they even use body parts from dead animals for protection!

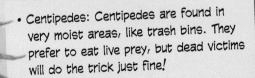

- Centipedes: Centipedes are found in very moist areas, like trash bins. They prefer to eat live prey, but dead victims will do the trick just fine!

FROM GARBAGE TO GOLD

Compost is a mixture of stuff that's decaying.

Some people don't just throw away food that's gone bad; they turn it into something useful! The food is put into an open bin outside. Certain insects, like millipedes, sow bugs, slugs, and snails, munch on the stuff and shred it into small pieces. Eventually, the decomposed garbage (called *compost*) will be put on soil to help new plants grow.

GARBAGE GRAZERS

COCKROACHES

Family: Blattidae

Species: More than 4,000 different
kinds (and close to 10,000
more still undiscovered)

Cockroaches have been around for more than 300 million years. They've lived for so long and changed so little that they're sometimes called *living fossils*.

Cockroaches have wings, but you'll rarely see them fly. Instead, they get around with the help of their strong legs.

Because its body is so flat, a cockroach can squeeze easily through small cracks when it needs to.

What does a cockroach eat? Just about anything— even wood!

AMAZING BUT TRUE!

Check out these cool facts about cockroaches:

- A cockroach can lose its head and still live for up to a week.

- A cockroach's eyes help it to see in all directions.

- A cockroach's brain takes up space in both its head and body.

- A giant burrowing cockroach weighs 1 oz. (28 g)— more than any other roach.

- A cockroach can go without air for 45 minutes.

- A cockroach leaves chemical "messages" in its dung for other cockroaches.

- A cockroach can survive for more than a month without food.

- A cockroach prefers moving around at nighttime when it's dark.

- A cockroach can survive without food by licking the back of a postage stamp.

ROACHES

DUNG BEETLES

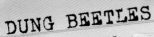

Genus: *Scarabaeus*

Species: *sacer*

They say you are what you eat. In that case, you already know what the dung beetle eats—poop! Dung beetle *grubs* (babies) chew dung while adults suck out its nutrients.

Dung beetles have two sets of wings, one in front and one in back. Their back wings help them to fly. Their front wings are called *elytra*. These wings act as shields, protecting the dung beetle's other set of wings and the rest of its body.

THREE'S COMPANY

There are three kinds of dung beetle:

1. Rollers: These dung beetles roll dung into balls. They store them for snacks to be eaten at a later time.

2. Tunnellers: Tunnellers do what you might imagine they would do with their dung balls— they bury them in tunnels.

3. Dwellers: Dwellers live inside of their dung balls.

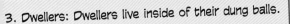

A dung beetle has "teeth" on its legs. The teeth help the insect to burrow and roll dung balls.

Dung beetles work hard for their dung. They use their super-keen sense of smell to find it, and then they roll it into a ball. Sometimes, they'll even fight over a ball of dung. To these critters, dung is like gold!

Poisonous Predators

Many insects fight their enemies with *venom* (poison).
Venom can harm their victims and sometimes cause death.

Some insects are venomous, and others are poisonous. A
venomous insect has poison in its body and injects it into
its prey. A poisonous insect has poison in its body, but it
can't deliver it. An animal that eats a poisonous insect
will get sick or even die.

Check out this chart to see how some common stingers rate.

STINGER	SCHMIDT PAIN INDEX RATING
Sweat Bee	1
Fire Ant	1.2
Bald-faced Hornet	2
Yellowjacket	2
Honeybee	2
Red Harvester Ant	3
Paper Wasp	3
Tarantula Hawk	4
Bullet Ant	4

Ouch!
As you may already know, some insect bites and stings hurt a lot! But
did you know that there are numbers to rank how much a bite or sting
really hurts a victim? The numbers are part of a system called the
Schmidt Pain Index. Bites and stings are ranked between 1 and 4. A
sting or bite that ranks a 4 is the most painful.

GOTCHA!

Meet five of the world's most skillful predators:

- **The Giant Centipede:** This 1-ft.- (3-m-) long killer grabs its prey with its hollow claws. Then, it injects it with venom.

- **The Potter Wasp:** Good luck hiding from the potter wasp! A potter wasp that finds a caterpillar hiding inside of silk-bound leaves will immediately cut open a hole in the caterpillar's "shield," quickly sting and kill it, and then bring it home as a meal for its babies.

- **The Robber Fly:** Robber flies are fearless. They chase wasps and bees. They even tackle dragonflies that are more than twice their size! Robber flies stab their victims with saliva that numbs them and turns their insides into liquid. Then, the flies slurp up their meal.

- **The Spitting Spider:** The spitting spider sneaks up on its victim before "spitting" at it. Once its victim is glued to the ground, the spitting spider paralyzes it with venom. Then, it can begin its feast.

- **The Yellow Crazy Ant:** Yellow crazy ants are called crazy because of the jerky way they move when predators approach. Sometimes yellow crazy ants get together in big groups. They spray enemies with a burning chemical called *formic acid*. The acid is strong enough to cause chemical burns on human skin or blindness if it gets into a person's eyes.

POISONOUS PREDATORS

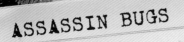

ASSASSIN BUGS

Family: Reduvilidae

Genus: *Zelus*

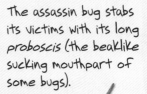

The assassin bug stabs its victims with its long *proboscis* (the beaklike sucking mouthpart of some bugs).

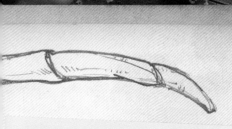

Assassin bugs have two big bright spots on their backs. Sometimes predators confuse the spots with eyes and turn the other way.

An assassin bug can spit at prey as far away as 1 ft. (3 m). Because its saliva is so toxic, a victim may die in just 10 seconds.

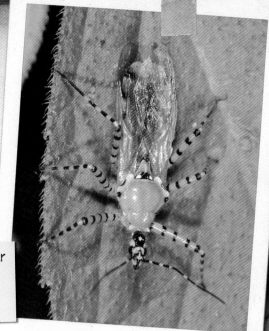

Assassin bugs are fierce hunters. That's how they got their name! They grab their victims with lightning-fast speed. Then, they poison them.

Assassin bugs grab their prey using the sticky pads on their legs. Each pad is covered in thousands of little hairs that stick to a victim's body.

Some assassin bugs measure as long as $1\frac{1}{2}$ in. (3.8 cm). Assassin bugs aren't usually afraid of larger insects.

FIRE ANTS

Family: Formicadae

Genus: Solenopsis

Some fire ants are red, and almost all have a reddish-brown colored head.

Fire ants live in large groups called *colonies*. Together, they build mounds and feed on plants, seeds, and occasionally larger insects such as crickets.

Sometimes, fire ants will seek out and kill small animals. First, they bite their victims. Then, they sting them again and again, injecting them with strong venom.

A fire ant's venom burns like fire. Ah, so that's how it got its name!

SCRAM!

The red fire ant first arrived in the U.S. in the 1930s. Since that time, they've caused lots of problems! More than 300 million acres (1.2 million sq. km) of land are infested with these ants. These bugs are a farmer's worst nightmare. They destroy equipment by biting through wires and sometimes even kill farm animals.

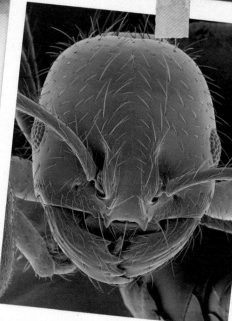

Here's looking at you!

As if one fire ant isn't enough to deal with, sometimes a swarm of ants will fight an enemy. These mass attacks usually happen when a mound has been disturbed.

An ant's two antennae are called *feelers*. They detect chemicals in the air and on the ground.

WASPS

Genus: *Vespula*

Species: *C. vulgaris*

Believe it or not, wasps don't have nearly as many hairs as their bee relatives!

There are two kinds of wasps. Solitary wasps spend their time alone. Social wasps live in colonies, like ants. A single wasp colony can be made up of as many as several thousand wasps!

Different wasps play different roles within their colony. Colonies include queens, workers, and drones.

Only female wasps sting. Males don't have stingers. A female wasp can sting again and again. Unlike a honeybee, she won't die after stinging a victim just once.

WACKY WASPS

Check out these cool wasp facts:

The paper wasp chews on—what else?—wood and paper.

- The bald-faced wasp's nest is football-sized and hangs from a branch.

- The potter wasp builds its nests out of mud.

Would you believe that some wasps actually lay their eggs inside the bodies of other insects? Caterpillars and tarantulas, beware!

- The yellow jacket wasp is, not surprisingly, usually yellow and black.

- The female tarantula hawk wasp's stinger can be $\frac{1}{3}$ in. (0.8 cm) long.

BEES

Superfamily: Apoidea

Species: About 20,000 different kinds throughout the world.

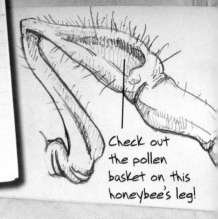

Check out the pollen basket on this honeybee's leg!

Bees are close relatives of ants and wasps. Bees live everywhere you can think of—except for Antarctica.

Bees taste with their antennae. A bee has thousands of taste buds and can smell its food from miles away.

As with wasps, only female bees sting. Males don't even have stingers! When a female honeybee stings, her stinger gets stuck inside of her victim. Then, when she tries to fly away, her stinger breaks off. Soon, she will die. A female bumblebee is a little luckier than her honeybee cousin—stinging won't cause her to die. In fact, she won't even lose her stinger in the process!

Honey is actually nectar that a bee eats and then spits back up!

There are nine different families of bees.

HONEYBEES VS. BUMBLE-BEES

- Unlike honeybees, bumblebees produce small amounts of honey—only enough to feed their young.

- Honeybees may swarm when a trespasser gets near their nest. Bumblebees, on the other hand, live in small nests and almost never swarm.

- Honeybees are much more aggressive than bumblebees.

To bee or not to bee?

BEES

SPIDERS

Family: Blattidae

Class: Arachnida

Species: Close to 40,000 kinds throughout the world

Like many spiders, this one has eight eyes.

Spiders aren't insects—they're arachnids.

A spider's body is made up of two body parts and eight legs. Unlike many of the insects in this book, spiders don't have wings.

Most spiders have eight eyes, but some have only two. The way a spider's eyes are arranged depends on its species.

Some spiders use venom to kill their prey.

There are more than 100 different families of spiders.

In 1973, two spiders were taken into outer space. Why? Scientists wanted to see what their webs might be like when spun in zero gravity! What did they discover? The webs created in outer space were finer than the ones created back at home. Also, while Earth webs are usually consistent, the space webs were thicker in some places and thinner in others.

LET'S MEET SOME OF THESE EIGHT-LEGGED CRITTERS.

- **The Assassin Spider:** Assassin spiders are excellent hunters. They have long jaws and enormous fangs. Their long necks help them to attack victims from far away.

- **The Crab Spider:** The crab spider looks like a crab. Its front legs are extra-strong so it can grab its prey, which finds it difficult (and sometimes impossible!) to escape.

- **The Golden Wheel Spider:** The golden wheel spider is a natural born gymnast. When it needs to make an escape, it flips onto its side and cartwheels away.

- **The Ogre-faced Spider:** This spider traps its prey inside of a silk net. At the end of each night, it rolls up its net and enjoys dinner.

- **The Portia Spider:** The Portia spider takes an uninvited spot within another spider's web. There, it makes the same type of harmonic sound a trapped insect might make for several days—until the curious host comes out to investigate—at which time it quickly kills its prey.

- **The Trapdoor Spider:** The trapdoor spider waits inside of its tunnel until a passing insect falls through its trap door. Dinner is served!

Superfamilies: Scorpionoidea
(thin-tailed scorpions)
and Buthoidea
(thick-tailed scorpions)

Species: More than 1,000 kinds
throughout the world

A scorpion uses its crablike claws to trap its prey.

Some scorpions are born with two tails!

Like spiders, scorpions have eight legs. At the end of its legs are claws called *pedipalps*. A scorpion's tail has six segments. Its stinger is on its last tail segment.

Before using its stinger, a scorpion will first try to make enough noise to scare away its predators.

Some people say the smaller a scorpion's pincers are, the more deadly its sting. A scorpion with large pincers doesn't have the deadliest sting. Why not? Because its enormous pincers are usually strong enough to kill all by themselves!

DID YOU KNOW?

A scorpion glows in the dark when ultraviolet light is shined upon it. Scorpion hunters carry UV lights into the desert with them at night in order to catch their eight-legged specimens.

Home Invaders

When you picture insects, green leaves and dirt probably come to mind. But some insects prefer your home to the great outdoors! Check out these pests that you might find in your very own living room, or—eek!—in your bedroom or kitchen!

Centipedes: Most house centipedes have 15 pairs of legs. Centipedes are excellent escape artists. They can move quickly along floors, up walls, and even across ceilings!

Firebrats: Firebrats like it hot—around 100°F (38°C)! Look for these pesky critters inside boiler rooms, around ovens, and near hot-water heaters and pipes.

Midges: Midges are small, mosquitolike flies. Adult midges gather by porch lights in big groups called swarms, sneaking inside homes whenever doors are opened.

Moths: Most moths are *nocturnal,* which means they're more active at night. And they really like lights! They make small circles around their light sources over and over.

Silverfish: Silverfish actually feed on the glazed surfaces of photographs! If photos aren't available, they will munch on paper or wood instead.

Springtails: A springtail moves by snapping a hooklike structure on the bottom side of its belly against the ground, propelling it forward across the floor.

TAKE THAT!

Some exterminators use electronic pest repellers to get rid of bugs. These devices give off sounds that only the little critters can hear. The sounds make it difficult for the insects to communicate with one another and redirects them back outside, where they belong.

EARWIGS

Class: Insecta

Order: Dermaptera

These are an earwig's forceps. Forceps open to seize prey and close to trap it.

Earwigs are also sometimes called *pincher bugs*. They can be found all over the world. They have long, flat brown bodies. The largest earwig is the St. Helena earwig, which can be as long as 3 in. (7.6 cm).

An earwig has two pairs of wings. The front wings are short and leathery and they are sometimes called *skin wings*. Even though earwigs have wings, they don't fly much.

Earwigs are nocturnal and like to hide in places that are dark and damp. Where might you find an earwig? Try looking inside wall cracks. Sinks are also favorite earwig hangouts.

HOW CORNY!

Earwigs damage many kinds of flowers and vegetables. Have you ever come across a cob of corn missing several of its kernels? That very well may have been the handiwork of an earwig. Ragged leaves are also signs that an earwig may have paid a plant a visit.

There are 28 different families of earwigs.

Some people claim that earwigs hide inside human ears and lay their eggs in there. The good news? It's not true.

EARWIGS

TERMITES

Order: Isoptera

Species: Close to 30,000 different kinds throughout the world

There are seven different families of termites.

cool!

Termites look a lot like ants. In fact, some people call them *white ants*. Like ants, termites live in colonies. Some colonies have several queens.

Termite colonies live inside nests. You can find termite nests in trees, underground, and sometimes even in mounds above the ground. The mounds look a lot like anthills.

Termites belong to different groups depending on what they eat. Wood-eating termites can cause major damage to homes. By the time a homeowner discovers termites, the damage has usually been done.

People in central and southern Africa sometimes put nets around lamps to trap termites. The termites' wings are removed, and then the insects are roasted or fried and enjoyed as a snack!

TERMITES ARE TRULY AMAZING CREATURES.

Need proof? Check out this list of true termite fun facts.

- One termite colony may have millions of members.

AWSOME!

- Termites recognize their own kind—and intruders!—by smell.

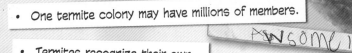

- Some termite mounds can be as tall as 25 ft. (7.5 m)!

- Termites sometimes use dung to build tunnels that hide them when they have to cross open spaces.

- A termite might bang its head against a tunnel wall to call for help.

AND CROSS

TERMITES

Name That Bug!

By now, you're a true insect (and non-insect) expert! Based on what you've learned, can you identify the three creatures shown in the following SEM images? For each image, you've been given three clues.

1. What am I?
- Some of my relatives have as many as 750 legs.
- To escape from enemies, I burrow into the ground.
- I might spray you in the eyes or mouth with a toxic liquid.

_____

2. What am I?
- I look a lot like a crab.
- My front legs are super-strong.
- I'm not an insect—I'm an arachnid.

crab ~~spider~~ spider

3. What am I?
- I wave my arms in the air when I'm trying to hitch a ride.
- I sometimes drink my victim's blood for four straight days.
- When I have eaten my fill, I fall to the ground.

_____

How to Use Your Microscope

How to view an object:
Place it against the clear lens protector. Adjust the focus by moving the microscope up and down a little bit. Hold the microscope steady to keep the image sharp and clear.

How to clean your microscope:
When the lens on the eyepiece gets dirty, gently blow the dust off of the lens. You can also wipe both ends with an eyeglass cleaning cloth. Keep your microscope in a clean, dry place.

Things you can look at with your microscope:

hair
feathers
fingernails
insects
fish scales
fabrics

flower petals
leaves
crystals
rocks
wood
your skin

Bugging Out

Okay, so you've learned about all kinds of awesome bugs, and you've figured out how to use the microscope that came in your kit. What's next? It's time to put your bug-hunting skills to work!

Here are a few tips for finding the little critters:

Look under:
- Stones
- Leaves
- Logs
- Boards
- Porches

Be sure to visit:
- Wood piles
- Flower beds
- Shallow waters
- Tree stumps
- Mud puddles

Try looking:
- After a rainfall
- In the evening
- During picnics
- When hiking
- While gardening

One Final Thought

Collecting insects can be fun, but don't forget that they're living creatures. Make sure to take extra-good care of them! If you disturb an insect in its home environment, return it to where you found it in exactly the same condition. And be very careful! Some bugs have a venomous sting or bite! And avoid swarms, or you might get more than you bargained for. Happy hunting!